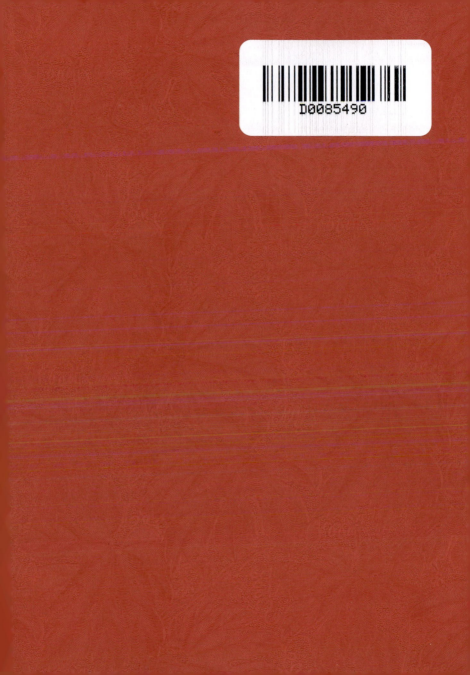

ANIMALS

THEIR PAST AND FUTURE

Originally published as:

ANIMALS

THEIR PAST AND FUTURE

BY
G. H. PEMBER, M.A.

HODDER AND STOUGHTON
LONDON NEW YORK TORONTO

ANIMALS

THEIR PAST AND FUTURE

The classic theological treatise on animal rights

G. H. PEMBER

Republished by Cross Reference Imprints

David W. Hill, Ed.

Animals: Their Past and Future
The classic theological treatise on animal rights
by G. H. Pember; David W. Hill, Ed.
© 2003 by David W. Hill, Cross Reference Imprints. All Rights Reserved.
Originally published by Hodder and Stoughton
2003 edition published by Cross Reference Imprints
PO Box 7126, Louisville, KY 40257-0126
For information on media interviews, please contact the publisher.

Available to retailers through all major wholesalers. Special discounts on bulk
orders are available to qualifying institutions. Call (502) 897-2719 for more info.

Cover and interior design by Pneuma Books, LLC.
For more information, visit www.pneumadesign.com/books

Printed in the United States by Thomson-Shore Inc.

10 09 08 07 06 05 04 03 02   5 4 3 2 1

Publisher's Cataloging-in-Publication
(Provided by Quality Books, Inc.)

Pember, G. H. (George Hawkins)
    Animals: their past and future: the classic
theological treatise on animal rights / G.H. Pember. –
2003 ed.
    p. cm.
    Includes bibliographical references and index.
    LCCN 2002114195
    ISBN 0-9725139-0-6

    1. Animal welfare–Biblical teaching. 2. Animal
rights–Biblical teaching. 3. Animals in the Bible.
I. Title.

BS680.A5P46 2002   241'.693
                          QBI02-200807

*Dedicated with gratitude
to Donald R. Metcalf,
a dear friend and brother.*

Table of Contents

Preface

This essay by eminent nineteenth-century British scholar and Bible expositor George Hawkins Pember was originally issued by Hodder and Stoughton of London as a pamphlet with no publication date. Its few pages and narrow focus set it apart from the imposing volumes that comprise the body of Pember's work.

Its brevity notwithstanding, this remarkable treatise stands as a model of the author's unassailable scholarship and courageous determination to examine social issues in the light of biblical truth.

The problem of humankind's indifference to the suffering of animals is, arguably, graver today than in Pember's time. The author's unadorned appeal to the Bible for wisdom in this matter may appear simplistic to some in an age of moral relativism. Yet it is precisely by his simple deference to scriptural authority that Pember succeeds in transcending the muddle of emotionalism that so often accompanies debate of "animal rights" issues and precludes enlightenment much beyond personal opinion and the dictates of tradition.

Although Pember assumes the reader's familiarity with certain biblical themes and persons, his argument is by no means addressed uniquely to the "churched." Non-believers may find corroborated here truths they have long held intuitively, without the benefit of Scripture. Bible believers, on the other hand, may find their traditional beliefs challenged by the radical thesis that God's great redemptive work does not have humankind as its sole focus, but that the destinies of man and beast have, from the beginning, been intertwined.

I hope that all readers will glimpse in the pages that follow a deeper vision of God's profound and abiding love for *all* His creation and of the part each of us is privileged to play in His unfolding plan.

David W. Hill
2002

ANIMALS

THEIR PAST AND FUTURE

"Thy judgments are a great deep;
O Lord, thou preservest man and beast."

Some two or three generations have already passed by since society awoke to the consciousness of duties lying before it ; and began, with ever-increasing energy, to devote itself to the redress of grievances and the furtherance of numerous projects for ameliorating the conditions of human life. And, in the course of subsequent years, many admirable results have been effected. Oppression has been checked, abuses removed, and the hours of labour curtailed; education has been placed within the reach of all; workhouses and prisons have been reformed; sanitary matters and the dwellings of the poor have received much attention; and countless schemes of benevolence have been organised and carried out.

In so active an age it might have been expected that the kindly feelings of men would not be exclusively attracted to the members of their own race, but that some few thoughts, at least, would be bestowed upon their four-footed and feathered friends. And such, indeed, has been the case, much to the benefit of beast and fowl. Yet the movement in their favour has hitherto been but partial; we still see around us a very prevalent indifference to the treatment of animals, an apathy which sometimes changes into enthusiasm over the deliberate torture of a living subject, if it be but affirmed that the human race may derive some little advantage from the process.

It is with a wish to deprecate such an in-differentism that we write the following pages, confining our remarks, however, to a single aspect of the question. We shall not search for the many arguments and appeals which might be found in the relations sub-sisting between man and the helpless crea-tures subjected to his will, but shall restrict our inquiry to this one point—Whether there are in the Scriptures any plain statements or hints which ought to influence our tone and behaviour towards animals.

Certainly, if we desire information re-specting them, we must turn to revelation;[A] for we can discover but little without it. Our own eyes will readily teach us that they are affected by such emotions as joy and grief, pleasure and disgust; while careful observa-tion will further prove that they are more or less guided by reason, and influenced by love, envy, jealousy, pride, and other passions, in much the same manner as ourselves. But at this point our investigation is checked: what these creatures really are, we have no means of finding out; nor can we tell whence they came, or whither they are going. If, however, we consult the inspired page, we shall be enabled to learn something both of their past history and of their future destiny.

As to their past history, we can at least ascertain that, like the human race, they have fallen from a higher condition, and are now lying under a ban. This may be inferred from the sentence pronounced upon the serpent, "Thou art cursed above all cattle, and above every beast of the field"—words which evidently imply a curse involving the whole animal kingdom. But the truth is revealed in plain terms by the apostle Paul, when he tells us that the creation—*ἡ κτίσις*—was made subject to vanity; that all living organisations[B] have, against their will—*οὐχ ἑκοῦσα*—become slaves to corruption, and are, therefore, for the present, doomed to experience decay, pain, and death.[1]

Of this great change we seem able to trace many consequences. Take, for instance, the fact that the world now abounds with carnivorous animals, that one creature lives upon the flesh of another, that incessant destruction saddens the face of nature. It was not so in the beginning; for then the green herb was the sole food of beast and fowl,[2]

---

1. Rom. viii. 20.
2. Gen. i. 30.

even as it shall be—so we are told—in future time, after the curse has been removed.[3]

Again, when the serpent addresses Eve with articulate words, she betrays neither surprise nor suspicion. May we not fairly infer that animals then possessed some power of speech ? Such a supposition is from every side probable ; for if they were given to Adam as vassals, it is but reasonable to conclude that, so long as he remained in a state of innocence and retained his sovereignty, there would be a means of intelligent communication between himself and his willing subjects.

And this inference is, perhaps, strengthened by an expression in the history of Balaam.

---

3. Isa. xi. 6—9.

"The Lord," we read, "opened the mouth of the ass,"[4]—a manner of describing the miracle which, at least, favours the idea that the creature was originally endowed with speech, and is abnormally dumb.

Once more; in the thirty-ninth chapter of Job, it is recorded of the ostrich that "God hath made her to forget wisdom"[5]—for such is the literal rendering of the text—words which need no unnatural forcing to make them signify that she was not always the foolish bird she now is.

Other hints might be adduced pointing in a similar manner to the great fact that a change for the worse has befallen the animal

---

4. Numb. xii. 28.
5. Job xxxix. 17.

---

world. But the Bible contains still more; it discloses in no obscure terms God's glorious purpose for the future of the ruined creature, and, at the same time, the tender care with which He at present regards it. Of this statement we will now proceed to give some proof.

The first chapter of Genesis teaches us that God created six great tribes to inhabit our earth—viz., the fish of the sea, the fowl of the air, the cattle, the creeping things, the beasts of the earth, and man. Now the first five of these tribes were placed under the dominion of the sixth; nevertheless, only three of them are mentioned as having been specially brought to Adam to be named—the cattle, the fowl of the air, and the beasts of the field.[6]

---

6. Gen. ii. 19, 20.

These three, then, appear to be distinguished from the two which remain, and, as we shall presently see, are destined to be with man upon the renewed earth.

No reason is given for the omission of the fish and of the creeping things: but possibly these may be in some way included among the three tribes which are expressly mentioned. Yet there are two facts which may point in an opposite direction. For in the renewed earth there will be no more sea; and it was through the medium of the serpent, the head of the creeping things,[7] that sin entered into our world.

---

7. Or, if not so originally, he was, at any rate, degraded to this position—a circumstance which would not tend to set the tribe in a more favourable light.

Shortly after Adam had named the creatures of the three tribes, he transgressed, involving himself and the creation in ruin, and
was driven out of Paradise. But upon looking
back regretfully through the closed gates of
the garden, he saw four glorious forms stand-
ing near the Tree of Life. They were the
Cherubim, whom God had so placed that
they could take of the fruit of the tree; but
around them He had set a threatening circle
of flame, which forbade access to any other
living being.

If we would search for the meaning of
these appearances, we must learn to avoid
two common mistakes;—

First, the Cherubim are not angels, but
are the "Living Creatures" described in the
first chapter of Ezekiel and the fourth of the
Apocalypse.[C] In the latter book they are ex-

pressly distinguished from angels; for John[D] says, " And I heard a voice of many angels round about the Throne, and the Living Creatures and the Elders."

And, secondly, they had nothing whatever to do with the action of the flaming sword, which, as the Hebrew explicitly states, " kept turning itself to guard the way to the Tree of Life."

Premising these cautions, we may now go on to consider the one point in the description of their form and appearance with which we are at present concerned—the fact that their heads were those of a man, a lion, an ox, and an eagle. In seeking an interpretation for this symbolism, we must remember that God Himself has classified the animal kingdom, and named the three honoured tribes, beasts of the field, cattle, and fowls of the air. Now while the man's head obviously indicates the human family, the lion is the king of wild beasts, the ox the chief of domestic animals—in Eastern countries at least, and the eagle the first of birds. It would thus seem that the Cherubim are in some way or another connected with four of the great earth-tribes which lost their first estate through Adam's sin.

And this idea is confirmed when we investigate the probable meaning of their name. For כְּרֻבִים divides readily into כְּ־רֻבִים, which in literal English would signify "as the many," and thus imply that the Cherubim were representative beings.

Such an explanation is in beautiful accord with the present context; for if it be correct, the appearance of the Cherubim must have been to Adam a sweet consolation and a glorious prediction of the future. Because of his transgression he had just been thrust out

from the garden of delight, and the ceaseless
flashing of the fiery sword taught him that he
could no more put forth his hand and take of
the Tree of Life. But *within* the guarded circle stood the four living creatures ; and in
their representative forms he doubtless per-
ceived a promise that God would yet devise
means to fetch home again His banished
ones, to restore both man and beast to the
privileges of the Tree of Life.

If we now pass on to the times of Noah,
we shall meet with a very striking corrobora-
tion of the view we have taken—a corrobora-
tion, indeed, which may almost be said to
amount to a demonstration of its truth. For the
covenant which God made with Noah after the
deluge is indited in the following terms ;—
"And I, behold, I establish My covenant with
you, and with your seed after you, and with

every living creature that is with you, of the fowl, of the cattle, and of every beast of the earth with you."[8]

Here the four tribes indicated by the Cherubim are specially and distinctly mentioned as being all of them heirs to the promises of the Noachian covenant. Moreover, we may further observe, that, whereas the sign of the covenant was the rainbow, so whenever, in after time, the real Cherubim appear, the rainbow is always visible above them.[9] Thus the promise of God remains sure, that He will never again smite any more every living thing, as He did in the days of Noah; and that promise is made to beast as well as man.

8. Gen. ix. 9, 10.
9. See Ezek. i. 28; Rev. iv. 3, 6.

A little later in the sacred history we find the Cherubim in the tabernacle ; for Moses was commanded to have their forms inwoven in the inner of the four curtains which covered it,[10] so that they were seen in the place of God's habitation. The same forms adorned also the veil of blue, purple, and scarlet, which divided the Holy of Holies from the Holy Place.[11] Thus both the ceiling and the four sides of each compartment of the tabernacle exhibited representations of Cherubim. And, most significant of all, their figures in gold were to be placed upon the Mercy-seat of the Ark, one on either side.

10. Exod. xxvi. 1.
11. Exod. xxvi. 31-33.

But here, again, we have to protest
against a popular error. In almost every di-
agram of the Ark—the only honourable ex-
ception that occurs to us at the moment is
the plate in Parkhurst's Hebrew Lexicon[E]—
the Cherubim are depicted as angels. There
is, however, not the slightest warrant for
such a refusal of hope to the animal creation. In each description of the celestial
beings, the heads of the other creatures are
mentioned as well as that of a man. This is
true even in John's great vision of the Heavenly Places, where both the altars appear,
and where the laver expands into a sea of
glass like unto crystal, and seven torches of
fire are burning before the Presence.[F] For
there at the foot of the rainbow-encircled
Throne, sat the Cherubim, in forms which
brought to remembrance the four tribes of

earth with whom God's covenant is made.
And since there is little doubt that this
scene reveals to us some of those heavenly things from which Moses received his
patterns, it is scarcely probable that the
Cherubim on the Ark would differ in shape
from the real Living Creatures described by
the apostle.

If, then, this point be conceded, and there
is not, in counterpoise to the arguments used
above, a word in Scripture to disprove it, let
us for a moment consider what is likely to be
the meaning of the appearance of such forms
upon the Mercy-seat.

The Ark was the Ark of the Covenant,
above which hovered the Shechinah;[G] none,
therefore, could dare to stand before it save
those who were perfect in God's sight and
acceptable to Him. Had any other ventured

to approach the awful Presence, the flaming sword would have quickly revealed itself, and a blasted corpse, like that of Nadab or Abihu,[H] have fallen to the ground.

But why should the creature be thus sternly debarred from communion with the Creator ? Because God is holiness and justice as well as love, and the creature has sinned and broken the law of the Creator. That law, " the bond written in ordinances that was against us," was placed within the Ark of the Covenant, and completely covered by the golden lid, or Mercy-seat, which represented the atoning merits of Christ. His perfect righteousness is the one thing which the piercing eye of God never penetrates. Accordingly, in the symbol which we are considering, while the Mercy-seat concealed

---

the violated law from the Divine justice,
the Cherubim[12] rested upon the lid in safe-
ty, and should have continually reminded
men of two facts. First, that God keeps
ever before Him the memorials of those
tribes which He has promised to save.
And, secondly, that those that are represented by the Cherubim shall be delivered
from sin and corruption, and be empow-
ered to dwell in the light of God's presence, through the atoning sacrifice of the
Lord Jesus.

---

12. Many insist that the Church is indicated by this symbol, and defend their opinion by urging that the Cherubim were made of beaten gold, and of one piece with
the Mercy-seat which is Christ. But they have forgotten that others, beside Christian believers of the present age, will ultimately be united to Christ. The prophecy contained in the Cherubim looks, far beyond the

But the Cherubim represent the animal creation as well as man; therefore, the animal creation will also be redeemed with man.

If it be objected that our inference is too important, too subversive of ordinary theological teachings, to be allowed from arguments based upon a symbolism which we may have misinterpreted; we reply, that, in the Old Testament, the mysteries of redemption were ever veiled in symbolism; but, that in the New the salvation of the creature is set before us in plain and unmistakable terms.

glorification of the Church, to that dispensation of the fulness of the times in which God has purposed to sum up all things in Christ, the things in the heaven, and the things upon the earth (Eph i. 10).

A sufficient proof of this may be found in the well-known passage contained in Rom. viii. 19-24. There Paul declares that " the earnest expectation of the creation waiteth for the revealing of the sons of God "; for the day when, in a moment, in the twinkling of an eye, the vile bodies[13] of His elect shall be changed into the likeness of Christ's glorious body. And that then the time will have come for " the creation itself also " to " be delivered from the bondage of corruption into the liberty of the glory of the children of God."

---

13. I use this familiar expression from our English Bible ; but the Greek, it is scarcely necessary to remark, has " the body of our humiliation."

Such will be the end of the groaning and travailing in pain together of the whole creation. And, like ourselves who have the first-fruits of the Spirit, the animal creation is saved by hope; for it was subjected to vanity "in hope."[14]

With such direct predictions before us, we need not fear to accept in their most literal sense those passages—such as Isa. xi. 6-9, lxv. 25; Ezek. xxxiv. 25, 28; Hos. ii. 18—in which it is said that hereafter the wolf shall lie down with the lamb, the lion eat straw like the ox, and the asp and cockatrice become the playmates of children. For when the hour of re-

---

14. Compare the twentieth and twenty-fourth verses of the eighth chapter of Romans.

demption has come, and sin is removed from man, all that is hurtful in the animal creation will also disappear; nay, the brute earth itself will be relieved from the curse.

It is not, therefore, strange that, in describing the great redemption scene at the close of this age, John should say, " And every creature which is in heaven, and on the earth, and under the earth, and such as are in the sea, and all that are in them, heard I saying, Blessing, and honour, and glory, and power, be unto Him That sitteth upon the Throne, and unto the Lamb, for ever and ever."[15] Nor yet that the Psalmist, enraptured with his vision of the coming King, should exclaim;—

15. Rev. v. 13. Compare Psalm cxlviii.

"Let the heavens rejoice, and let the
      earth be glad;
Let the sea roar, and the fulness thereof;
Let the field be joyful, and all that is
      therein:
Then shall all the trees of the wood
      rejoice
Before the Lord;—for He cometh,
For he cometh to judge the earth.
He shall judge the world in
      righteousness,
And the peoples in His faithfulness."[16]

For the Lord will return to destroy the
works of the Devil, and to reveal that glory of
God which has been for long ages effaced by

---

16. Psalm xcvi. 11-13.

them; so that all living creatures will be re-
stored once more to the peace and harmony
of the Garden of Eden, and the ground will
again bring forth an abundant supply for
their need.

Seeing, then, that the great Creator has
so gracious a purpose in regard to the future of animals, we should with reason ex-
pect to find some proofs of present care for
them, scattered here and there, at least, in
His revelation: nor shall we be disappoint-
ed if we search.

In the very first chapter of Genesis we
are made to understand, that, while the fruit-
bearing trees were assigned to Adam for sus-
tenance, every green herb was given for
meat to the beasts of the field and the fowls
of the air. After the fall of man, his food was
changed, and he, too, was compelled to have

recourse to " the herb of the field."[17] But
God's care for the humbler creatures did not
cease: for, as the Psalmist says, "He causeth
the grass to grow for the cattle, and the herb
for the service of man."[18]

In process of time the wickedness of
men became so great that God was compelled to sweep every living thing from the
face of the earth. But before doing so, He
took measures to preserve a nucleus for a
new population ; and these measures included, not only eight human beings, but
also a pair, at least, of each family in the
animal kingdom, that they, too, might prop-
agate their kind in the recovered world.

17. Gen. iii. 18.
18. Psalm civ. 14.

They were saved in the same ark with Noah and his family; and after they had been for some time shut up in their gloomy coffin, we are told that " God remembered Noah, and every living thing, and all the cattle that was with him in the ark."[19]

Nor was the beast forgotten amid the pealing thunders of Sinai ; for even there proclamation was made that the Sabbath-rest should not be confined to man, but should bring ease and repose to the cattle also.

A like consideration for the inferior crea-ture is shown in the history of Balaam, when speaking of the ass, the angel says, " Unless

19. Gen. viii. 1.

she had turned from me, surely now also I had slain thee, and saved her alive."[20]

So, too, Jonah's foolish anger at the respite of Nineveh was rebuked with the words, "And should not I spare Nineveh, that great city, wherein are more than sixscore thousand persons that cannot discern between their right hand and their left hand, and also much cattle ?"[21] God's pity for a hundred and twenty thousand infants and much cattle had saved the vast city.

A little later, when Habbakuk is denouncing the cruelty of the Chaldeans, and threatening a fearful retribution, he not only lays to their charge the blood of men

---

20. Numb. xxii. 33.
21. Jonah iv. 11.

and the violence inflicted upon the city and
its inhabitants, but also adds—if we render
correctly—" The outrage done to Lebanon
shall cover thee, and the devastation
among the beasts which terrified them."[1]
Thus, in reckoning up the ghastly tale of
crime, God had not forgotten that ruthless
felling of cedar and cypress, and burning of
forests, which had brought terror and destruction upon the wild beasts. Such acts
should fall back upon the perpetrators with
crushing weight, and overwhelm them.

We may appropriately close our appeal
to the Old Testament by citing the grand
distich from the thirty-sixth Psalm ;—

"Thy judgments are a great deep;
  O Lord, Thou preservest man and
    beast"

Unsearchable, indeed, are His judgments, like the great unfathomable ocean, and His ways past finding out! Who shall penetrate His mystery, until it be finished, and He be pleased to declare it ? But if we cannot now explain its marvelous workings, if at times we are perplexed, and begin to say with the heathen poet;—

"For dark and dusky wend the ways of
    His mind,
Not to be scanned by mortal eye,"

yet there is, at least, one thing which we know. We are in no uncertainty in regard to His purpose. It is to save multitudes alive out of this ruin of sin and death, to preserve— and to preserve what ? Not merely man, but man and beast.

In the New Testament, the Lord Himself affords us a wonderful insight into His Father's care for the inferior creatures. Upon one occasion, after reminding His hearers that sparrows were of such little account among men that two of them might be purchased for a farthing, He adds, " Not one of them shall fall to the ground "—that is, through being wounded, or frozen, or storm-smitten, or in any other way disabled—"without your Father."[22] The expression "without your Father," is very re-markable ; and there is no variation in the reading of any Greek MS., uncial or cursive. A few of the Latin versions, and one or two of the early Christian writings in which the verse is quoted, τῆς βουλῆς, "without *the will* of your Father" ; but this is merely a gloss. We must, therefore, omit it, and allow a full meaning to the text as it is ;—"Not a sparrow falls to the ground without the presence and support, as well as the will, of your Heavenly Father."

In a similar passage, in the third Gospel, our Lord puts the reputed worthlessness of sparrows in a still stronger light. If you

22. Matt. x. 29.

bought two pairs, you would have a fifth bird thrown into the bargain. And no wonder: for even to-day in Palestine the little creatures may be seen sitting in chattering rows upon the house-tops, or swarming like small clouds over the cornfields, and are easily caught for the market by children. "Are not five sparrows sold for two farthings? And not one of them is forgotten in the sight of God."[23] But if the great Creator has such tender care for these insignificant beings, with what mind is He likely to regard the thoughtlessness or brutal treatment to which His marvelous handiwork is so ceaselessly subjected by man ?[J]

Strange, too, as it may seem, the Bible certainly does appear to attribute to animals

23. Luke xii. 6.

themselves the power of appreciating, to some extent at least, the love and care of God; for they are often represented as looking up to Him in a manner which suggests that they have their way of petitioning Him to supply their need. "The young lions," says the Psalmist, "roar after their prey, and seek their meat from God."[24] And again, "He giveth to the beast his food, and to the young ravens which cry."[25] So, too, Joel, in describing the ruin of his land, exclaims;—"The beasts of the field cry also unto Thee: for the rivers of waters are dried up, and the fire hath devoured the pastures of the wilderness."[26] And the

24. Psalm civ. 21.
25. Psalm cxlvii. 9.
26. Joel i. 20.

Almighty Himself, in His wonderful address
to Job, when the soul of the patriarch was re-
belling against a necessary discipline, asks;—
"Who provideth for the raven its food, when
its young ones cry unto God ?"[27]

Such, then, are some of the Scriptural
revelations and hints touching the present
condition and future destiny of animals. But
how little consideration do they obtain; nay,
by how few are they barely known! The
greater part even of our educated classes do
not seem to bestow a thought upon the subject; and if their attention should at any time
be drawn to it, are wont to dismiss the whole
question with some such summary remark
as that the Bible speaks of "the beasts that

27. Job xxxviii. 41.

perish." Or, perhaps, they reply, that those creatures cannot be worth much consideration whose spirits at death go "downward to the earth," and are dissolved in the dust, instead of ascending upward like the spirits of men. Well, if there are other portions of Scripture throwing a different light upon those which we have quoted above, we must, of course, be content to modify our inferences; but let us at least examine the two passages to which allusion has just been made, and which are ever the readiest weapons in the hands of our opponents.

The first of them occurs in the forty-ninth Psalm, where, with a slight variation, it is twice used as a refrain in the twelfth and twentieth verses. In our English version the twelfth verse runs as follows;—

"Nevertheless man being in honour
        abideth not:
He is like the beasts that perish."

Now our first remark upon this verse is, that
the Hebrew word for "perish" literally means
"are reduced to silence." Hence, no less an authority than Fürst[K] translates, "the beasts that
are dumb." The word is, therefore, a somewhat
insecure foundation for an argument.

But even if we waive this, and take the passage as it stands in our version, we are again
met with the fact that the verb נִדְמָה is used
of men as well as of beasts.[28] Whatever, then,
is here predicated of beasts may also be true
of men.

---

28. See Hosea x. 7, 15, and Isa. vi. 5.

And, lastly, the best rendering of the verse is probably that of Delitzsch[L] who makes both " man " and " beasts " the subject of the verb;—

> " Man being in honour abideth not:
> He is like the beasts : they—*i.e.*, both
>   of them—perish."

So much for the first quotation. The second is found in Eccles. iii. 21, a verse which, according to all ancient translators and many modern commentators—among whom we may mention Delitzsch and Zöckler[M]—is incorrectly rendered in our Bibles, and should take an interrogative form. It occurs in one of those sceptical[N] meditations which indicate the phases through which the mind of Solomon passed during his fruitless striving

---

after happiness, and of which there are several examples in the Book of Ecclesiastes before we come to its noble conclusion. The paragraph begins with the eighteenth verse, where, in reference to what has gone before, the king affirms that God delays His decisive judgments in order that He may sift the sons of men, and give them an opportunity of observing that in themselves, and apart from Him, they have no advantage over the beasts. For the same fate awaits both man and beast alike. Death is inevitable to every living thing; all are hastening to the same place, and will soon be mingling their dust in the great common graveyard, their mother earth. There is, indeed, the possibility that man and beast do not share the same fate after death ; but that is uncertain, and involves a question that has never been answered: for—

"Who knoweth in regard to the spirit of
the sons of men, whether it goeth
upward; or in regard to the spirit of
the beast, whether it goeth downward to the earth ?"

Such appears to be the meaning con-
veyed by the Hebrew text of this passage.
But were we to admit the sense of the English version and regard the verse as an affir-
mation, it would even then furnish no proof
that the spirits of animals are annihilated. To
a Hebrew mind, the expression "goeth downward to the earth" would signify " goeth
downward to Hades "—that place of depart-
ed spirits which is often mentioned as being
in the lower parts of the earth, in the heart
of the earth ; to which Korah, Dathan, and
Abiram,[O] went down alive when the earth

opened her mouth; and from which the spirit of Samuel came up out of the ground.[P]
Even in this case, then, no more would be
affirmed of animals than is said of men in
Psalm ix. 17—

> " The wicked shall return to Hades,
>   Even all the nations that forget God."

It is thus clear that neither of these passages permits us to think slightingly of the
animal creation, as though its tribes had
been called into existence for the sole purpose of administering to our pleasures, and
were destined ultimately to vanish into eter-
nal nothingness. The conclusions which we
have deduced above remain intact, and
should powerfully influence our treatment of
creatures which appear, like ourselves, to

have a future before them, and which are
doubtless made to play no unimportant part
in our discipline here below.

Our powers over them are almost unlim-
ited, and they are indisputably our inferiors
in every way: these two facts are often adduced as an unanswerable proof that it is
right to treat them with any cruelty, provided that by their sufferings we can secure
some advantage for ourselves or our race.
Were this logic true, it would be somewhat
disquieting; for we may reasonably suppose
justice to be the same throughout the uni-
verse, and there are beings more powerful
than we. But the great Creator Himself, tow-
ering so high above us in wisdom and might
that the distinction between ourselves and
the beasts becomes relatively inappreciable,
set us no example of selfish disregard for in-

feriors when He gave His Only-begotten Son
for the life of the world.

There are two great tasks appointed for us in this present age: we must learn to obey and to rule. Every human being is frequently exercised in both of these lessons: all have to obey, and all, in some way or another, to rule. And these two things—that is to say, a willing submission to lawful authority from God downward, and a perfect self-restraint in exercising whatever power may be entrusted to us—comprise the whole duty of man. The first should be done with promptitude and cheerfulness; the second, with firmness, but with the tenderest consideration for those over whom we are set. Whenever we are called upon to rule, we should deal as we would wish God to deal with us.

Now one purpose obviously served by the inferior creation is to supply opportunities by which we may be exercised in this matter, and may show that we have not consented to the selfish maxim that might is right whenever interests or passions are concerned. And while these opportunities are useful to every one, there are many whose conduct under the temptation of power could scarcely be tested at all were it not for the presence of animals. The child with his cat or bird, the boy with his donkey, and the labourer with his dog or horse, should each be learning lessons of justice, kindness, and self-restraint. Nor is it less incumbent upon the man of science to admit the claims of other sentient creatures, and to confess that it is not lawful to pluck the fruit from every tree of knowledge.

Yet these truths are regarded only by a few, and countless cruelties—often, indeed, through thoughtlessness—are daily, nay hourly, perpetrated. This may, perhaps, seem a light matter, but we shall assuredly discover hereafter that the saying, " With what measure ye mete, it shall be measured to you again," applies to our dealings with beast as well as man. The scales of justice must be made even ; and, therefore, all unnecessary and wanton cruelty, too, if it become a habit, will be heard of again. For in that day—

> "When the Judge His seat attaineth,
>   And each hidden deed arraigneth,
>   Nothing unavenged remaineth."[Q]

Publisher's Notes

A. Scripture. Truth *revealed* in God's written word.

B. Organisms.

C. The last book of the New Testament, commonly re-
ferred to as *The Book of Revelation*; properly termed
The Revelation of Jesus Christ.

D. The Apostle John chronicled the apocalyptic vision
given him by Jesus Christ through the intermediary
of an angel on the Island of Patmos circa 93 AD; the
document is commonly called *The Book of Revelation*.

E. Parkhurst, John, 1728-1797, English lexicographer,
clergyman, educated at Clare Hall, Cambridge (B.A.
1748, M.A. 1752). Said to have been of a sickly con-
stitution, but heir to a considerable fortune which allowed him the leisure for theological study and to

write. This plate originally appeared in *An Hebrew and English Lexicon,* by John Parkhurst, M.A., published by G. G. and J. Robinson, Paternoster-Row, 1799. *See* illustration on p. 55.

F. *See* Revelation 4:3-8.

G. Or, *Shekinah.* The visible presence of God between the Cherubim on the Mercy-seat in the Tabernacle and in the Temple of Solomon. Exodus 40:34-38; I Kings 8:10-11.

H. Sons of Aaron, Levites, stricken dead by fire from heaven for not having sought God's instruction concerning the burning of incense in their ministration as priests. Leviticus 10:1-3.

I. *See* Habakkuk 2:17

J. Consider, in this regard, the telling parable spoken by Nathan the prophet which exposes King David's adultery with Bathsheba and his murder of her husband. II Samuel 12:1-10.

K. Fürst, Julius, 1805-1873, German, Orientalist, born in Zerkovo, Posen, of Jewish heritage; became professor at Leipzig in 1864; renowned for his mastery of rabbinical literature as demonstrated in his *History of Jewish General and Literary Culture in Asia* and *History of Biblical Literature and Hellinico-Judaic Letters* (1867-1870). *A Hebrew and Chaldee Lexicon to the Old Testament* is his only work available in English.

L. Delitzsch, Franz, 1813-1890, German Hebraist and exegetist; became Professor of Theology at Rostock in 1846, at Erlangen in 1850, and at Leipzig in 1867; one of the foremost theologians of the Erlangen School; a prolific writer, many of whose works have been translated to english.

M. Zöckler, Otto, 1833-1906, German, born in Grünberg, Upper Hesse; appointed Professor of Theology, University of Greifswald in 1866, where he remained until his death; a prominent Lutheran theologian and prolific writer.

N. Skeptical.

O. Korah, Dathan, and Abiram were Levites who rebelled against the God-given authority of Moses and were dramatically judged. Numbers 16:8-35.

P.   Terrified by the prospect of defeat by an imposing
     Philistine army, Saul, Israel's first king, enjoins a
     medium to summon the spirit of the dead prophet
     Samuel for counsel. I Samuel 28:1-24.

Q.   *See* Revelation 20:11-13.

The Cherubim of Glory mentioned on page 17 of this
book. *Also see* publisher's note E.

Bibliography

Delitzsch, Franz. *Behold the Man*. Translated by Elizabeth C. Vincent. New York, 1888.

———. *Biblical Commentary of the Book of Job*. Grand Rapids: W. B. Eerdmans Publishing Co., 1949.

———. *Biblical Commentary on the Prophecy of Isaiah*. Translated from the 4th ed. Edinburgh: T. and T. Clark, 1910.

———. *Biblical Commentary of the Proverbs of Solomon*. Translated by M. G. Easton. Grand Rapids: W. B. Eerdmans, 1950.

———. *Biblical Commentary on the Psalms*. Vol. 3. London: Hodder and Stoughton, 1888-1894.

———. *Commentary on the Epistle to the Hebrews*. Grand Rapids: W. B. Eerdmans, 1952.

————. *Commentary on the Song of Songs and Ecclesiastes.* Edinburgh: T. and T. Clark, 1891.

————. *A Day in Capernaum.* Toronto: Funk and Wagnals Co., 1892.

————. *A Hebrew New Testament of the British and Foreign Bible Society; A Contribution to Hebrew Philology.* Leipzig: Dorffling and Franke, 1883.

————. *Jewish Artisan Life in the Time of Our Lord.* London: S. Bagster and Sons, 1877.

————. *Messianic Prophecies in Historical Succession.* New York: Scribner's Sons, 1891.

————. *New Commentary on Genesis.* 5th ed. New York: Scribner and Welford, 1889.

————. *Old Testament History of Redemption.* Edinburgh: T. and T. Clark, 1881.

————. *Solemn Questions Addressed to Hebrews of Culture.* New York: The American Sabbath Tract Society, 1890.

————. *A System of Biblical Psychology.* Edinburgh: T. and T. Clark, 1890.

———. *Talmudic Notes on St. Paul's Epistle to the Romans.* Gettysburg, Penn., 1881.

Fürst, Julius. *A Hebrew and Chaldee Lexicon to the Old Testament.* Leipzig: B Tauchnitz, 1885.

Parkhurst, John. *The Divinity and Pre-existence of Our Lord and Saviour, Jesus Christ, Demonstrated from Scripture;....* London: T. Payne and Son, 1787.

———. *A Greek and English Lexicon to the New Testament: in Which the Words and Phrases...to this Work is Prefixed a Plain and Easy Greek Grammar....* London: J. R. Major, 1851.

———. *An Hebrew and English Lexicon, Without Points... to This Work are Prefixed an Hebrew and a Chaldee Grammar Without Points.* London: G. G. and J. Robinson, 1799.

———. *A Methodical Hebrew Grammar Without Points....* London: W. Faden and C. Dilly, 1765.

———. *A Serious and Friendly Address to the Reverend Mr. John Wesley, in Relation to a Principal Doctrine Advanced and Maintained by Him and His Assistants....* London: J. Withers, 1753.

Zöckler, Otto. *The Book of Job. A Rhythmical Version with Introduction and Annotation by Professor Taylor Lewis.* New York: Scribners, 1902.

———. *The Book of the Chronicles. Theologically and Homilitically Expounded by Dr. Otto Zöckler.* New York: Scribners, 1901.

———. *The Book of the Prophet Daniel. Theologically and Homilitically Expounded.* New York: Scribners and Co., 1890.

———. *The Cross of Christ: Studies in the History of Religion and the Inner Life of the Church.* London: Hodder and Stoughton, 1877.

———. *Ecclesiastes; or Koheleth.* New York: Scribner, 1871.

———. *The Lutheran Cyclopedia.* New York: C. Scribner and Sons, 1899.

———. *The Song of Solomon.* New York: Scribner/Armstrong, 1873.

Biographical Notes on
G. H. Pember

George Hawkins Pember was born in 1837. He was educated at Cambridge University where he took his M.A. in Classics at age twenty-six. Upon his conversion to Christ, Pember determined to devote his scholastic talents to a close and comprehensive study of the Scriptures for the benefit of God's people. His penchant for meticulous scholarship, extensive knowledge of ancient cultures, and keen spiritual insight combined to produce works of a quality and depth with few parallels in Christian expository literature.

G. H. Pember died in 1910, leaving a rich legacy of reclaimed spiritual truth, upon which subsequent reformers such as J. N. Darby, Watchman Nee, G. H. Lang, and T. Austin-Sparks would build.

A rewakening of interest in Pember's writings was signaled by Kegel Publication's reissue of *Earth's Earliest Ages* in 1975. By 1998 Schoettle Publications had reprinted the majority of Pember's foundational works concerning the kingdom, prophecy, and the rapture.

"He was preeminently a teacher of teachers, and one of the best exponents of prophetic Scripture during his period, so rich in great teachers of the Word of God."

—*G. H. Lang*

"...a writer foremost in scholarship, in expository insight, in literary clarity, who had the added gift of interpreting facts in the light of Scripture.... One of the deplorable facts of today is the disappearance of these giants, and even of their works, with few if any to take their place...."

—*D. M. Panton*

"...a book [*Earth's Earliest Ages*] of distinct and conspicuous mark on the exhaustless theme of Scripture Prophecy."

—*United Presbyterian Magazine*

"One of the most valuable expositions of prophecy [*Earth's Earliest Ages*] ever published...masterly, discriminating, scholarly... eloquent...."

—*Prophetic News*

Other Works
by G. H. Pember

Earth's Earliest Ages. Grand Rapids: Kregel Publications, 1975.

The Great Prophecies of the Centuries Concerning Israel and the Gentiles. Haysville, N.C.: Schoettle Publishing Co., 1998.

The Church, the Churches and the Mysteries; or, Revelation and Corruption. Haysville, N.C.: Schoettle Publishing Co., 1998.

The Great Prophecies of the Centuries Concerning the Church. Haysville, N.C.: Schoettle Publishing Co., 1998.

The Great Prophecies Concerning the Gentiles, the Jews, and the Church of God. Haysville, N.C.: Schoettle Publishing Co., 1998.

The Lord's Command. Haysville, N.C.: Schoettle Publishing Co., 1998.

Mystery Babylon the Great. Hayesville, N.C.: Schoettle Publishing Co., 1998.

Theosophy, Buddhism, and the Signs of the End. London: Hodder and Stoughton, 1892.

The Antichrist, Babylon and the Coming Kingdom. Toronto: S. R. Briggs, (n.d.).

Internet Resources

Following is a list of websites related to the proper treatment of animals. Many of these websites are maintained by secular organizations; their views may not be compatible with Christian ideology. The publisher is not affiliated with any of these websites and takes no responsibility for the information or opinions expressed. This list is provided for your information only.

Stop Animal Abuse
A letter-writing service that helps you make a difference for animals.
hometown.aol.com/letters4animals

All Creatures.Org
Sponsored by The Mary T. and Frank L. Hoffman Family Foundation. Dedicated to cruelty-free living through a vegetarian-vegan lifestyle according to Judeo-Christian ethics. Unconditional love and compassion is the foundation of our

peaceful means of accomplishing this goal for all of God's creatures, human or otherwise.
http://www.all-creatures.org/

HSUS (Humane Society of the United States)
The Humane Society of the United States makes a difference in the lives of animals here at home and worldwide. The HSUS is dedicated to creating a world where our relationship with animals is guided by compassion. We seek a truly humane society in which animals are respected for their intrinsic value, and where the human-animal bond is strong.
http://www.hsus.org/

ASPCA (American Society for the Prevention of Cruelty to Animals)
The ASPCA exists to promote humane principles, prevent cruelty and alleviate fear, pain and suffering in animals. Learn how we fight animal cruelty, lobby for animal welfare and care for abandoned and abused animals.
http://www.aspca.org/site/PageServer

Animal Concerns Community
The Animal Concerns Community is a project of the EnviroLink Network, a non-profit organization which has been providing access to thousands of online environmental and animal rights/welfare resources since 1991.

This community serves as a clearinghouse for information on the Internet related to animal rights and welfare.
www.animalconcerns.org/

Animal Rights Online
We have decided to devote our spare time to help the lives of animals. The animals are very dear to our hearts, and it saddens us whenever we learn of any cruelty, exploitation, and abuse toward them.
www.geocities.com/RainForest/1395/

The Moral Status of Animals
Part of the Ethics Update website. Designed primarily to be used by ethics instructors and their students. It is intended to provide updates on current literature, both popular and professional, that relates to ethics.
http://ethics.acusd.edu/Applied/animals/

Animal Rights FAQ
There are hundreds of AR-related organizations scattered around the globe. In addition, there are many vegetarian and vegan groups. This FAQ is already too long to list all of these groups. This FAQ gives only AR-related groups in the United States and the United Kingdom.
http://www.animal-rights.com/

Animal Rights Web Ring
This web ring was designed to link sites together that concern animal rights, endangered species, vegetarian/vegan, animal respect, or animal welfare related information. I feel that respecting animals and the earth is the first step towards treating animals equally.
www.geocities.com/RainForest/Vines/2326/ring.html

ISAR (International Society for Animal Rights)
ISAR was founded in 1959 to expose and end the injustice and exploitation of animals and the suffering inflicted on them. Since that time ISAR has become a leader in the fight for Animal Rights, living up to the commitment in its name.
www.isaronline.org/

Yahoo! News: Animal Rights Issues
news.yahoo.com/fc ?tmpl=fc&cid=34&in=world&cat=animal_rights

Animal Aid
Animal Aid is the UK's largest animal rights group and one of the longest established in the world, having been founded in 1977. We campaign against all forms of animal abuse and promote a cruelty-free lifestyle.
www.animalaid.org.uk/

Index